LOVELAND PUBLIC LIBRARY

000312497

D0538767

WEDDING DAYS

CELEBRATING MARRIAGE

ANITA GANERI

PETER BEDRICK BOOKS

NEW YORK

INTRODUCTION

In each of the world's six major religions, the most important times in a person's life are marked by special ceremonies. These are a bit like signposts on the journey through life, guiding a person from one stage of their life to the next. They also give people the chance to share their beliefs and their joys or sorrows, whether in celebrating a baby's birth, the change from child to adult, a wedding, or marking and remembering a person's death. For each occasion, there are prayers to be said, presents to give and receive, festive food to eat and stories to tell. Customs and ceremonies vary in different parts of the world. This book looks at just some of them.

WEDDING DAYS

This book examines how people from the Hindu, Buddhist, Sikh, Jewish, Christian and Muslim faiths celebrate a wedding. Marriage is a joyful time when a couple show their commitment to each other and set out on their new life together. Each faith has its own wedding customs, many of which date from ancient times.

In this book dates are written with BCE and CE, instead of BC and AD which are based on the Christian calendar. BCE means 'Before the Common Era' and it replaces BC (Before Christ). CE means 'in the Common Era' and it replaces AD (Anno Domini 'in the year of our Lord').

 This is the Hindu sacred symbol 'Om'. It expresses all the secrets of the universe.

 This wheel is a Buddhist symbol. Its eight spokes stand for eight points of the Buddha's teaching.

 This Sikh symbol is called the 'Ik onkar'. It means: 'There is only one God'.

 The Star of David is a Jewish symbol. It appears on the flag of Israel.

 The cross is a Christian symbol. It reminds Christians of how Jesus died on a cross.

 The star and crescent moon are symbols of Islam.

CONTENTS

THE SEVEN STEPS

Most Hindus marry someone chosen for them by their families, although the boy and girl must agree with their parents' choice. A priest looks at the couple's horoscopes to make sure their personalities are well suited. Then a lucky day is chosen for the ceremony, a hall is hired and wedding invitations are sent out to family and friends.

Getting ready

It takes a Hindu bride many hours to get ready for her wedding. She wears a beautiful silk sari which is embroidered with gold, and lots of heavy gold jewellery including many bracelets. Traditionally, a wedding sari is red because red is the colour of blood and so of life itself. The bride's hands and feet are decorated with delicate patterns, painted in mehndi (henna), a red dye from plants.

The day of the wedding

On the day of the wedding, there are 15 different rituals to be performed. When the bridegroom arrives, the guests hurry to greet him, singing songs and placing flower

It can take several hours to paint the beautiful patterns of mehndi (henna) on a bride's hands and feet.

garlands around his neck. He then sits next to the bride, under a large canopy. This is where the religious ceremony takes place. The bride's father places her right hand into the groom's right hand to show that he is giving his daughter in marriage.

The whole ceremony is conducted by a priest who reads from the sacred texts. These are written in Sanskrit, an ancient Indian language. The bride and groom follow the priest's instructions but they do not speak to each other.

A wedding necklace

To show that she is married, a Hindu bride wears a black and gold necklace, called a mangala sutra. She also paints a red mark on her forehead while her husband is alive.

A Hindu bride and groom

Loveland Public Library
Loveland, Colo. 80537
Withdrawn

Hindu weddings can be held in any suitable place, such as someone's house, a hall or in the open air. In India, special wedding gardens can be hired for the big day.

Joining the couple

For good luck, the priest sprinkles the couple with holy water, then he ties the groom's scarf to the bride's sari to show that they are joined together for life. The bride places her foot on a special stone, as prayers are said for her. She must now stand firm as a rock, and be loyal to her husband and his family.

Then it is time for the priest to light the sacred fire. The couple throw ghee (butter) and rice into the flames as offerings to the gods. In return, the priest asks the gods to bless their marriage and to bring them a long and happy life together.

The seven steps

The most important part of the ceremony comes towards the end when the couple take seven steps around the sacred fire. With each step they make a vow. These vows are for food, good health, wealth, good fortune, children, happiness and, finally, life-long friendship. The couple are now married.

The bride and groom throw offerings into the sacred fire in return for the gods' blessings. The priest reads from the scriptures and tells the couple what to do.

A new family

The wedding ceremony lasts for about three hours. Then the bride and groom pose for photographs and a great feast is held for all the guests. After the wedding, the bride leaves her home and goes to live with her husband's family. For Hindus, family life is very important. Many live in 'joint' families. This means that parents, grandparents, children, aunts, uncles and cousins all live together under the same roof.

How Rama won Sita

The god, Rama, and his wife, Sita, are seen by Hindus as a model married couple. This is the story of how Rama won Sita's hand.

Rama, the son of the king of Ayodhya, was handsome, strong and brave. He was also skilled at archery. One day Rama and his brother, Lakshman, saved a holy man from attack. To thank them, the holy man took the brothers to the court of King Janaka. The king was holding an archery contest, and the winner would marry his beautiful daughter, Sita. When his turn came, Rama shot a huge, golden bow that no one else could even lift. And this is how he won Sita's hand.

Rama and Sita

A BUDDHIST BLESSING

Buddhists celebrate weddings in different ways, according to the customs of the country in which they live. After their wedding, the couple may visit a monastery to be blessed by the monks. The monks do not take part in the wedding itself, and there is no special Buddhist wedding ceremony.

Wedding customs

In many Buddhist countries marriages are arranged by the two families. The wedding itself often takes place in the bride's home and is usually conducted by an uncle or male cousin. The couple may stand on a special platform, called a purowa. They exchange vows and have their right hands tied together with a silk scarf to symbolise their marriage. Afterwards, there is a wedding feast.

A Buddhist wedding in Thailand. The couple wear head-dresses joined by a thread to show that they are married. They offer flowers to the Buddha.

The Buddha's family

The Buddha was a nobleman's son by birth. He married his cousin, a beautiful princess called Yashodara, when he was just 16 years old. They had a son, called Rahula. When the Buddha was 29, he left his home and family to live as a monk and search for the meaning of life. He was later reunited with his family, and Rahula became one of his very first disciples.

The Buddha taught that family life was very important. He compared the members of a family to the trees in a forest. A tree growing on its own is easily blown over. But forest trees support and protect each other against the force of the wind. For the Buddha, the family meant more than just close relations. When a young man called Sigola came to the Buddha for advice, the Buddha told him to worship the six most important things in life – his parents, teachers, wife and children, friends, fellow workers and monks.

The sangha

The sangha is the worldwide community or family of Buddhists. Sometimes this means just Buddhist monks and nuns. Sometimes it means all Buddhists. For Buddhists, the sangha is one of the Three Jewels, the three most precious things in Buddhism. These are the Buddha himself, the dharma (his teaching), and the sangha.

A Sikh Wedding

A Sikh wedding may be held in the gurdwara, in a hall or in the bride's house. Wherever it is held, it must take place in front of the *Guru Granth Sahib*, the Sikh holy book. Most Sikh marriages are arranged by the couple's families.

In the gurdwara, the bride and groom sit facing the Guru Granth Sahib. *Before the ceremony, they are given a talk about the importance of marriage and of loving and respecting each other.*

Meeting and greeting

On the morning of the wedding, the first ceremony to be held is called milni, or meeting. This is the official meeting of the bride and groom's families. They drink tea and exchange gifts, such as lengths of cloth for making into turbans. Then everyone sits on the floor, facing the *Guru Granth Sahib*, and waits for the service to begin.

The wedding ceremony

The bridegroom usually wears a pink or red turban, and a long scarf, called a pulla, round his neck. The bride dresses in a red, pink or orange silk shalwar-kameez, a traditional suit made of trousers, a tunic and a long, flowing scarf. Both bow to the *Guru Granth Sahib* before sitting down. The marriage begins with readings and prayers from the holy book, and a talk about what marriage means. This is given by the person leading the marriage who may be any Sikh chosen by the family. Then the groom holds one end of his pulla and the bride the other, to show that they are being joined as husband and wife.

While the bride and groom hold each end of the groom's pulla (scarf), the musicians sing a hymn.

Family life

Marriage and family life are very precious to Sikhs. All the Sikh gurus (teachers) were married (except for Guru Har Krishnan who died when he was a child). In the 15th century the founder of the Sikh religion, Guru Nanak, taught that women were just as good as men, even though, at the time, many people did not agree. Sikhs still believe that men and women should be treated equally.

As the wedding hymn is sung, the couple walk around the Guru Granth Sahib, still holding the pulla which joins them together.

Four sacred circles

The most important part of the wedding ceremony is the reading of the Lavan, or wedding hymn. This was written by Guru Ram Das, the tenth Sikh guru (teacher), for his own daughter's wedding. You can read some of the words in the box. The four verses are spoken first, then sung. As each verse is sung, the bride and groom walk around the *Guru Granth Sahib*. When they have done this for a fourth time, they are married. The guests shower them with rose petals as a sign of congratulation. The ceremony ends with the reading of another prayer, called the Ardas, and the sharing of a bowl of karah parshad (a sweet food made of flour, sugar and butter) to show that everyone is equal in God's eyes.

The Wedding Hymn

This is the first verse of the Lavan, the Sikh wedding hymn:

'In this first circle, God has shown you the duties of family life.
Accept the Guru's word as your guide
And it will make you free from sin.
Meditate on the Name of God,
Which is the theme of all the scriptures.
Devote yourself to God and all evil will go away.
Blessed are those who hold God in their hearts.
They are always content and happy.'

Leaving home

After the ceremony comes the reception. The guests often give gifts of money, which they pin to the groom's shirt, and coconuts, which are symbols of good luck. Then they share a meal. Soon it is time for the bride to go to her husband's home where she will now live. As she leaves, the bride is given a handful of rice to throw over her shoulder. This is a way of wishing for the happiness of those who have come to see her off.

At the reception, the guests give money and other gifts to the couple. They place garlands of flowers around their necks as a sign of blessing.

Guru Ram Das

Ram Das married the daughter of the ninth Sikh Guru, Amar Das, and for many years helped his father-in-law in his work. When Amar Das died in 1574, Ram Das became the the tenth Guru. Ram Das is famous for composing the Lavan, the Sikh wedding hymn. He also laid the foundations for the city of Amritsar in India, the Sikhs' most sacred city.

Guru Ram Das (1574-81)

A SEAL UPON THE HEART

Jewish weddings usually take place on a Sunday. They are not permitted on a Saturday because this is the Shabbat, or holy day. The ceremony itself is usually held in a synagogue and is conducted by a rabbi, a Jewish religious leader and teacher.

A Jewish wedding takes place with the bride and groom standing under a huppah. The wedding begins with a reading from the scriptures.

A new roof

During the wedding ceremony the bride and groom stand under a canopy, called a huppah. The huppah represents the new home that the couple will share. It is closed on the top

for privacy but open on all sides as a sign that others are welcome inside. The rabbi reads from the scriptures and talks to the couple about the meaning of marriage. Then he takes a glass of wine, blesses it, and gives it to the bride and groom to drink, as a symbol of their shared joy.

The marriage contract

A very important document is now read out loud to the whole congregation. This is the ketubah, or marriage contract. It sets out the promises that the couple make to each other for a long and happy marriage. The bride and groom sign the ketubah in front of the rabbi and two other witnesses. Then the groom gives the bride a gold ring. Sometimes the ring is given before the ketubah is signed.

The bride and groom sign the ketubah (above) to show that they are both willing to enter into marriage. The ketubah is handwritten in Hebrew by a specially trained scribe (left).

Sarah and Abraham

Jews believe that a wedding ring has many different meanings. As well as being a symbol of marriage it also represents a new link in a long chain reaching back through the many generations of Jews to Abraham, the father of the Jews, and his wife, Sarah.

Breaking a wine glass

When the ketubah has been signed, the rabbi blesses the couple seven times, once for each of the seven days of creation. The end of the ceremony is very dramatic. A wine glass may be wrapped in cloth or tissue paper. Then the groom stamps on it and breaks it. This is a very ancient part of the ceremony. It is said to be a reminder of the destruction of the Jews' great Temple in Jerusalem, almost 2000 years ago. It shows the couple that there will be sadness as well as happiness in their future life together.

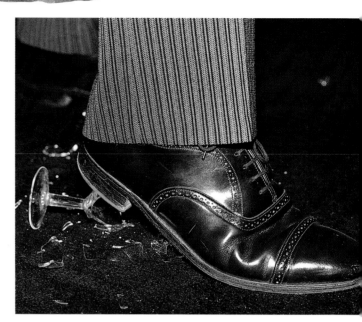

The wedding ceremony ends with the groom stamping on a wine glass to remember the destruction of the Temple in Jerusalem.

The Temple in Jerusalem

Jerusalem is the Jews' holiest city and the Temple was their holiest place of worship. The first Temple was built by King Solomon some 3000 years ago. It was a beautiful building, covered in gold. This Temple was destroyed by the Babylonians in 586 BCE. It was later rebuilt, only to be destroyed again by the Romans in 70 CE. Only one wall survived. This is called the Western Wall and is the most important place for Jews to go to pray.

At the reception, everyone joins in the dancing. Music and dancing are very important to make the bride and groom happy.

A happy occasion

As the bride and groom step out of the huppah, the congregation call out in Hebrew, "Mazal Tov! Mazal Tov!" which means 'good luck and congratulations'. The happy day ends with a reception, with lots to eat and drink, and plenty of music and dancing.

There are toasts and speeches to wish the couple well. The music at a Jewish wedding is often traditional. The musicians may play folk songs as well as tunes specially composed for the wedding.

Laws about food

In the *Torah*, the Jewish scriptures, there are many laws about food. Food that Jews may eat is called kosher. All fruit and vegetables are kosher. Jews may also eat meat from animals that chew the cud and have cloven hooves (hooves split in two), such as cows, sheep and goats. They must not eat the meat of pigs or rabbits. Fish with fins and scales are kosher but shellfish are not. Jews may eat chicken, turkey and duck but not meat from birds of prey.

A CHURCH WEDDING

Many Christians choose to get married in church and to ask for God's blessing on their commitment to each other. There are many different groups of Christians. Wedding customs vary from group to group and from country to country. But the service is always performed by a minister or priest and the most important parts of the ceremony are very similar.

The bride and groom kneel while the priest reads the words of the wedding service.

Getting ready

Before their wedding, the couple visit their minister or priest to discuss the arrangements for the day itself. They also talk about the meaning of the marriage service so that they understand the promises they will make to each other. There are lots of other things to be done, such as sending out invitations, organising the food for the reception afterwards, and deciding what to wear. Christian brides usually wear white or cream to symbolise modesty and purity.

In the church

On the day of the wedding, the groom and his Best Man arrive early at the church to greet the guests. The Best Man is a close friend of the groom. He helps the groom prepare for his wedding and looks after the wedding rings. Then everyone waits for the bride. She walks into the church and down the aisle with her father. Then she stands next to the groom, facing the altar. The service begins with a hymn and a reading from the *Bible.* After this, the congregation are asked if they know any reason why the bride and groom may not get married. If no one answers, the wedding can go ahead!

The marriage in Cana

Jesus and his disciples were once invited to a wedding in Cana, in Galilee. There was a great feast afterwards, with plenty of food and wine. But the wine soon ran out and the master of the house did not know what to do. In the corner of the room, stood six stone waterpots.

"Fill those pots with water," Jesus told the servants.

They filled them to the brim and took them to their master. When he poured some into his own cup and tasted it, a look of wonder filled his eyes. For Jesus had turned the water into wine. This was the first of Jesus's many miracles.

In the Orthodox Church, the couple drink wine from the same cup and wear crowns as a sign of God's blessing on their marriage and new life together.

Making vows

During the next part of the service, the priest asks the bride and groom to make their vows. They promise to love and protect each other, and to stay with each other faithfully, throughout their lives. As they make their vows they hold each other's right hands, as if they are shaking hands to seal an agreement. The bride's father agrees to give his daughter away in marriage, then the couple exchange rings as a sign of the promises they have made to

A special reading

This is part of a reading from the *Bible* which is very popular at Christian weddings because it talks about love:

'Love is always patient and kind. It envies no one. Love is never boastful or conceited. It is never rude or quick to take offence. Love does not keep score of wrongs. It does not gloat over other people's misfortunes but delights in the truth. There is nothing that love cannot face. There is no limit to its faith, its hope and its endurance. Love will never come to an end.' (1 Corinthians 13: 4-7)

each other. Many people wear their rings on the fourth fingers of their left hands. In ancient times, some people thought that a vein lead from this finger straight to the heart.

Husband and wife

The bride and groom are now husband and wife. There are prayers to ask God to look after them, a reading from the *Bible* or other Christian text and a talk by the priest about the importance of their marriage vows. The service ends with a blessing. Then the couple sign the marriage register, which makes their marriage official. The service is followed by a party, called a reception. After this the couple leave for a special holiday, called a honeymoon.

A beautifully decorated wedding cake. The bride and groom cut the cake together at the reception after the wedding. Traditionally, one tier (layer) of the cake is saved for their first baby's christening.

Throwing confetti

As the bride and groom come out of the church after their wedding, people often shower them with rice or confetti. This custom dates from Roman times when people threw almonds and other nuts. The nuts symbolised fertility and the hope that the couple would have healthy children.

Throwing confetti over the bride and groom

ALLAH'S BLESSING

Most Muslim weddings are arranged by the couple's families. But, according to the Shari'ah, or Muslim law, both the bride and groom are free to say no to their parents' choice. Weddings usually take place in the bride's home and are performed by any Muslim man.

A groom leaves his village in Pakistan to meet his bride. His face is covered as a reminder of the days when the bride and groom did not see each other until after the ceremony had been performed.

Fixing a dowry

Before the wedding takes place, the bride and groom's families have to fix a dowry. This is a sum of money or quantity of household goods that the groom's family must give to the bride. The dowry cannot be taken back. It is meant to give the bride some security if the marriage does not work out.

Sitting apart

By tradition, in Muslim weddings the bride and groom sit apart in separate rooms during the marriage ceremony. Two people are called forward as witnesses, one from the bride's family and one from the groom's. They hear the couple's vows and answers, and pass them on to the other partner. As the ceremony begins, the imam or another Muslim man recites from the

A worldwide family

A happy family life is cherished by Muslims because it is seen as a gift from Allah. All Muslims also belong to a much larger family, called the ummah. The ummah includes Muslims everywhere. They share the same values and beliefs, the same love of Allah and the Prophet Muhammad, and the same obedience to the *Qur'an*. This creates a very strong bond between Muslims, no matter where they live.

Qur'an, the sacred book of the Muslims, and gives a talk about the duties of marriage. He asks the couple three times if they agree to the marriage. The witnesses carry the answers from room to room.

The groom is given sweets and presents to welcome him into the bride's family.

The bride is also given sweets and gifts by the groom's family.

Promises and blessings

The bride and groom sign a contract which sets out the rules for their marriage. Then prayers are said for their future life together, hoping that they will be as happy as the Prophet Muhammad and his wife, Khadijah. The wedding ends with a celebration feast. This may be held in the bride's home or in a nearby hall. Here, too, men and women often sit apart.

The bride and groom sign a special marriage contract. Now they must obey the rules they have agreed for their lives together. The witnesses are also asked to sign the contract.

Teachings on divorce

The *Qur'an* says that a man may marry up to four wives – but only if he can treat them all equally. However, most Muslim men only marry one wife. In countries such as Britain and the USA, it is against the law to be married to more than one person at the same time.

If a marriage does not work out, the *Qur'an* says that Muslims are allowed to get divorced, but only as a last resort. First the couple must try to solve their problems. If this does not work, each must choose a friend or relation to give advice. If this still fails, they must wait for four months before they can end their marriage.

Muhammad and Khadijah

The Prophet Muhammad, who first taught people to follow Allah, married several times. But he loved his first wife, Khadijah, best of all. Khadijah was a wealthy widow. She heard about Muhammad's fairness and honesty and asked him to come to work for her. Khadijah was so impressed by Muhammad that she sent him a proposal of marriage. When Muhammad began preaching Allah's message for the world, Khadijah was the first to hear him and so she became one of his followers.

Food and drink

The *Qur'an* sets out many rules about food and drink. Food that Muslims are allowed to eat is called halal. Food that is forbidden is called haram. Fruit, vegetables and fish are all halal. Meat is halal only if an animal has been dedicated to Allah and killed in a certain way. Pork is always haram. Muslims are also forbidden to drink alcohol or to take drugs because they stop people doing their duty to Allah properly.

A shop selling halal food. Muslims have their own butchers where they can buy halal meat. The food eaten at a wedding feast, as every day, must be halal.

Fact Files

ॐ Hinduism

- **Numbers of Hindus:** *c.*732 million
- **Where began:** India (*c.* 2500 BCE)
- **Founder figure:** None
- **Major deities:** Thousands of gods and goddesses representing different aspects of Brahman, the great soul. The three most important gods are Brahma the creator, Vishnu the protector, and Shiva the destroyer.
- **Places of worship:** Mandirs (temples), shrines
- **Holy books:** *Vedas, Upanishads, Ramayana, Mahabharata*

☸ Buddhism

- **Numbers of Buddhists:** *c.* 314 million
- **Where began:** Nepal/India (6th century BCE)
- **Founder figure:** Siddhartha Gautama, who became known as the Buddha
- **Major deities:** None, the Buddha did not want people to worship him as a god.
- **Places of worship:** Viharas (monasteries or temples), stupas (shrines)
- **Holy books:** *Tripitaka* (*Pali Canon*), *Diamond Sutra* and many others

☬ Sikhism

- **Numbers of Sikhs:** *c.* 18 million
- **Where began:** India (15th century CE)
- **Founder figure:** Guru Nanak
- **Major deities:** One God whose word was brought to people by ten earthly gurus, or teachers.
- **Places of worship:** Gurdwaras (temples)
- **Holy book:** *Guru Granth Sahib*

✡ Judaism

- **Number of Jews:** *c.* 17 million
- **Where began:** Middle East (*c.* 2000 BCE)
- **Important figures:** Abraham, Moses, Isaac, Jacob
- **Major deities:** One God who created and rules over the world.
- **Places of worship:** Synagogues
- **Holy books:** *Tenakh* (Hebrew *Bible*), *Torah* (the first five books of the *Tenakh*), *Talmud*

✝ Christianity

- **Numbers of Christians:** *c.* 2000 million
- **Where began:** Middle East (1st century CE)
- **Important figure:** Jesus Christ
- **Major deities:** One God, in three aspects – as the Father (creator of the world), as the Son (Jesus Christ), and as the Holy Spirit
- **Places of worship:** Churches, cathedrals, chapels
- **Holy books:** *Bible* (Old and New Testaments)

☪ Islam

- **Numbers of Muslims:** *c.* 1000 million
- **Where began:** Saudi Arabia (*c.* 610 CE)
- **Important figure:** The prophet, Muhammad
- **Major deities:** One God, Allah, who revealed his wishes to the prophet Muhammad.
- **Places of worship:** Mosques
- **Holy books:** The *Qur'an*

GLOSSARY

Allah The Arabic word for God.

Ardas A prayer said at the end of all Sikh services. It remembers God and the teachings of the ten Sikh Gurus.

dharma An ancient Indian word meaning law or teaching. In Buddhism, it means the Buddha's teachings.

dowry Money or goods given to the groom by the bride's family, or to the bride by the groom's family.

gurdwara A Sikh place of worship.

Guru Granth Sahib The holy book of the Sikhs.

halal For Muslims, halal describes things that are allowed. Food that Muslims are allowed to eat is called halal.

haram Things that are forbidden to Muslims.

horoscope A chart showing the position of the stars and planets at the time of a baby's birth.

huppah A canopy under which a Jewish wedding ceremony takes place.

imam A Muslim who leads prayers in the mosque.

karah parshad A sweet shared out at Sikh services and ceremonies.

ketubah A Jewish marriage contract.

kosher Things which are 'fit' or 'proper'. Kosher describes food that Jews are allowed to eat.

Lavan The Sikh wedding hymn.

mangala sutra A necklace worn by a Hindu woman to show that she is married.

mehndi A red dye made of henna which is painted on to a Hindu bride's hands and feet.

milni A ceremony which takes place before a Sikh wedding when the bride's family officially meets the groom's family.

pulla A long scarf worn by a Sikh bridegroom.

Qur'an The holy book of the Muslims.

rabbi A Jewish religious teacher who leads the worship in a synagogue.

sangha The worldwide family of Buddhists, including monks, nuns and ordinary people.

Sanskrit An ancient Indian language. The Hindu sacred books are written in Sanskrit.

Shabbat The Jewish holy day. It lasts from sunset on Friday to sunset on Saturday.

shalwar-kameez A traditional suit worn by Sikh woman, made up of loose trousers, a long tunic and a long, flowing scarf.

Shari'ah Muslim holy law. Islamic law based on the *Qu'ran.*

Three Jewels The Three Jewels of Buddhism are the Buddha, the dharma and the sangha. They are called jewels because they are so precious.

Torah Jewish teaching; the first five books of the Hebrew *Bible.*

INDEX